Violin
Scales & Arpeggios
ABRSM Grade 5
from 2012

Why practise scales?

Welcome to this book of scales and arpeggios for Grade 5 Violin. Practising scales and arpeggios plays an essential part in developing a player's skills. Time devoted to these exercises within each practice session will improve many aspects of technique, such as co-ordination, string crossing, bow control, position changes and tone production. In addition, the sense of key and pattern acquired through familiarity with scales and arpeggios has several benefits: it speeds up the learning of new pieces, builds aural awareness, increases familiarity with the geography of the instrument, and helps develop fine intonation, evenness of line and quality of tone.

For the exam

Tempo

The candidate should aim for a tempo that achieves vitality of rhythm, controlled bowing, good intonation, and a clean, sonorous tone. Slurred patterns should generally be played with the whole bow, while separately-bowed examples should be played with a smooth *détaché*, using no more than half the bow length.

The given metronome marks indicate suggested *minimum* speeds for the exam. Candidates may feel that slurred requirements become more comfortable when played at a brisker tempo than examples with separate bows, such differences in speed being dependent on factors such as size of instrument and length of bow. Experienced teachers will know what their candidates are able to achieve safely, although it is important to avoid accurate yet laboured playing which demonstrates that the pattern has been memorized but lacks the musical fluency needed for a convincing result.

Fingering

The suggested fingerings in this book are neither obligatory nor exhaustive; any practical fingering that produces a good result will be accepted in the exam. The decision as to which fingering to adopt will vary between players, taking into account ease of performance, memorability, and the importance of changing position unobtrusively, and candidates should experiment to find solutions that work for them. (Examiners will not comment on the choice of fingering, unless it interferes with the musical outcome of the performance.) In this book, two fingering patterns are often given, one in standard print above the stave and the other in italic below.

On the day

All requirements must be played from memory. Examiners will usually ask for at least one of each type of scale or arpeggio required at the grade, and will aim to hear a balance of separately-bowed and slurred requirements.

The examiner will be looking for:
- good intonation across the pitch range
- an even and positive sense of rhythm
- accurate and fluent realization of the different types of scales and arpeggios
- confident, controlled, and consistent tone
- convincing negotiation of technical challenges such as string crossing, position changing, and co-ordination.

Rhythm patterns

For major and minor scales candidates may choose between two rhythm patterns: even notes *or* long tonic.

In this book, major and minor scales are presented in even notes first, followed by the same scales using the long-tonic pattern.

Reference must always be made to the syllabus for the year in which the exam is to be taken, in case any changes have been made to the requirements.

Published by ABRSM (Publishing) Ltd, a wholly owned subsidiary of ABRSM
© 2011 by The Associated Board of the Royal Schools of Music

GRADE 5
SCALES even notes *or* long tonic at candidate's choice

EVEN NOTES
separate bows *and* slurred
minor scales in melodic *or* harmonic form at candidate's choice

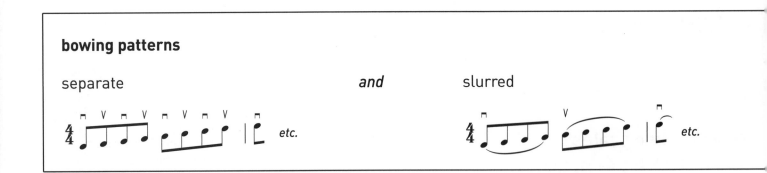

two octaves $\quad \downarrow = 80$

Db major
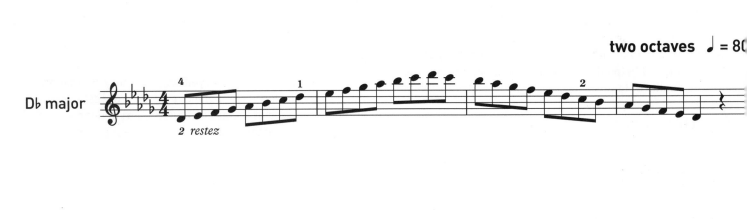

Eb major

F major

AB 3592

three octaves ♩ = 8...

G major

A major

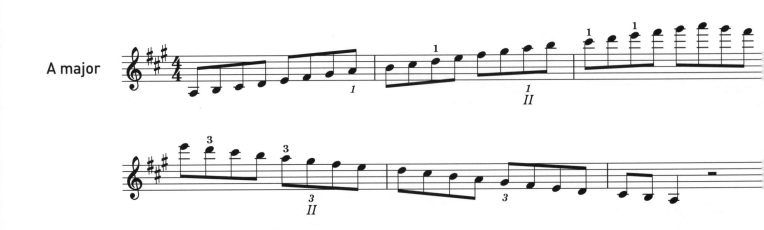

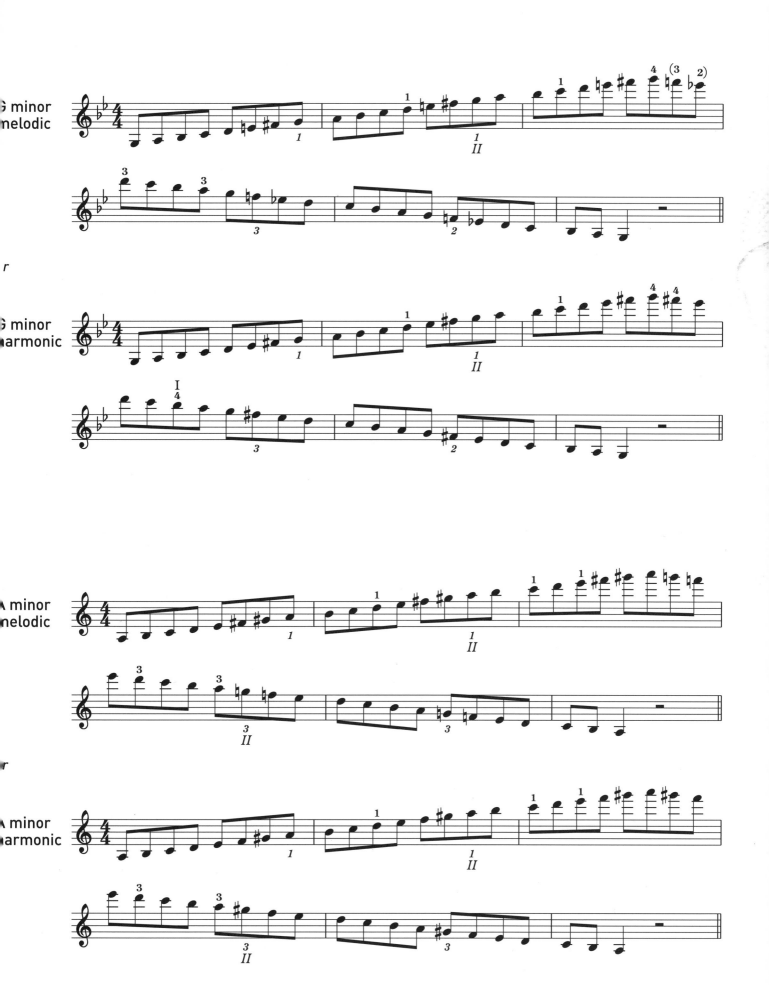

LONG TONIC

separate bows *and* slurred
minor scales in melodic *or* harmonic form at candidate's choice

bowing patterns

separate   *and*   slurred

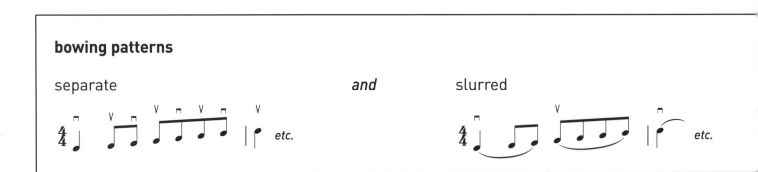

two octaves ♩ = 8

Db major

Eb major

F major

G major

A major

minor
melodic

minor
harmonic

minor
melodic

minor
harmonic

ARPEGGIOS
separate bows *and* slurred

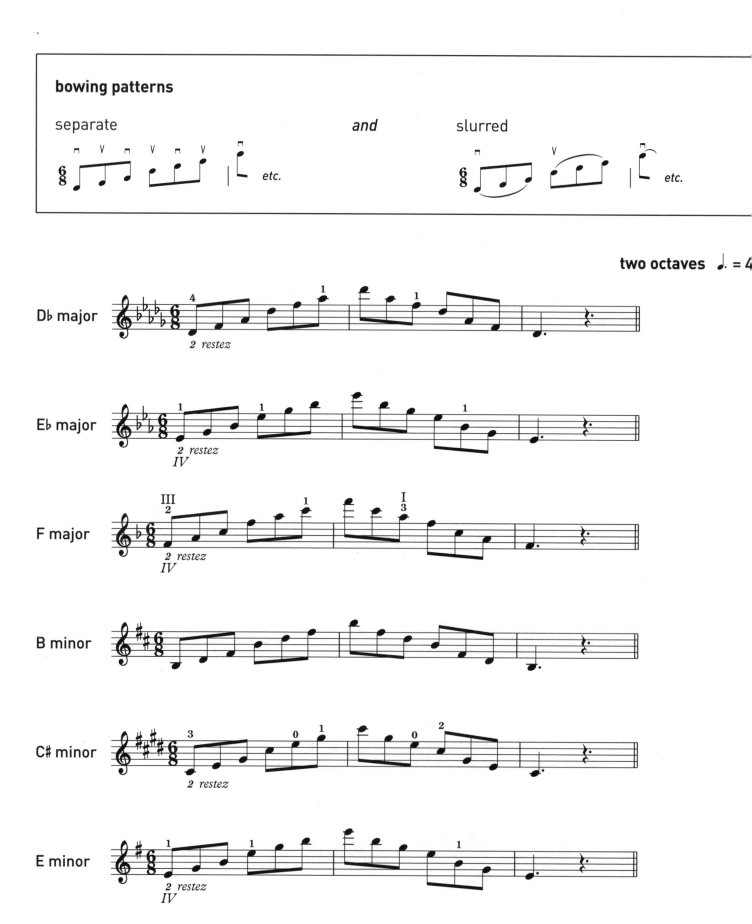

AB 3592

bowing patterns

separate   *and*   slurred

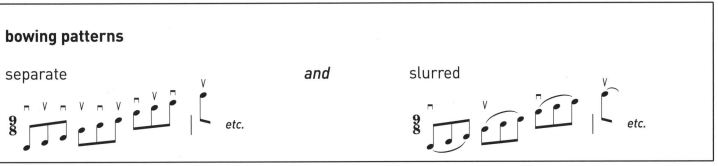

three octaves ♩. = 44

G major

A major

G minor

A minor

DOMINANT SEVENTHS

separate bows *and* slurred

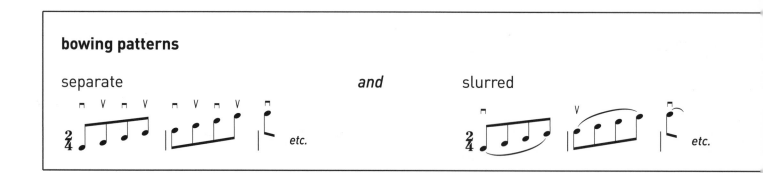

one octave ♩ = 6

in the
key of B♭

two octaves ♩ = 6

in the
key of C

in the
key of D

AB 3592

DIMINISHED SEVENTHS

separate bows only

bowing pattern

separate

one octave ♩ = 66

starting
on G

starting
on D

For practical purposes, the diminished sevenths are notated using some enharmonic equivalents.

CHROMATIC SCALES
separate bows *and* slurred

Music origination by Julia Bovee
Printed in England by Caligraving Ltd, Thetford, Norfolk

AB 3592

08/12